THE ACROPOLIS HISTORY

© KAPON EDITIONS, MARCH 2023
ISBN 978-618-218-016-7

KAPON EDITIONS
23-27 Makriyanni str., 117 42 Athens, Greece
T 0030 210 9235 098

RACHEL'S BOOKSHOP
22 Ploutarchou str., 106 76 Athens, Greece
T 0030 210 9210 983

www.kaponeditions.gr   info@kaponeditions.gr

PANOS VALAVANIS

THE ACROPOLIS HISTORY

Where Man and the Gods Meet

ILLUSTRATION: Costas Theocharis

KAPON EDITIONS

TRANSLATION: Dimitrios Doumas

Contents

PREFACE

The Acropolis and its Museum invite us on an imaginary journey through time: It is worth joining the adventure not only because of the monuments and works of art we will encounter but also because, through them, we will attempt to approach the people who inspired, created and lived them.

This is what makes Archaeology so fascinating: On the one hand, it gives life and breath to monuments and, on the other, it seeks to find human presence behind every work. The endeavour of the architect and the labourer behind a building, the inspiration of a sculptor that gives rise to a statue, the hard work of an ordinary slave behind a heavy and arduous task. The Acropolis with its Museum and monuments will offer us many such opportunities.

Our visit will try to answer simple and more complex questions on a number of issues ranging from the technical means by which the buildings were constructed, to the deeper reasons that led to their creation. However, our reward will not only be the knowledge and profound joy which great art offers, but also our ongoing contact with the past.
A past that is not just "ours", but forms part of the common heritage of mankind.

Our guides in this journey will be a veteran archaeologist and his 12-year-old studious nephew that keeps asking questions all the time out of his desire to learn and grasp everything! They are accompanied by the owl of Athena, the goddess of wisdom, that assists them as a flying guide.

ATHENS THEN AND NOW

— We know that ancient Athens was a great city. But how big was it actually? Was it as big as it is today?

— As you know, nowadays Athens is a conurbation that, with its central and remote districts, sprawls across the entire Attica. The image of the city in Antiquity was quite similar: However, the ancient city, the *asty* (urban centre), built around the Acropolis, was much smaller, occupying roughly the same area as today's historic centre.

Yet, I must remind you that ancient Athens was the capital only of the city-state of Athens. As is the case today, people also lived in around 140 larger or smaller settlements, called *demes*, spread all over the surrounding countryside, from Eleusis to Oropos and from Acharnae to Sounion.

— These days, the city's population is 4,000,000. Do we know how many the ancient inhabitants were?

— A lot less! Throughout Attica lived approximately 300–400,000 people, which makes up 1/10 of today's population. Of them, only 20-25,000 people were actual Athenian citizens, namely men who exercised their political rights and participated in governing bodies, such as the *Ekklesia tou Demou* (Assembly) and the *Boule* (Council of citizens), or held office as *archontes* (magistrates). If we assume that each citizen had a wife and three children, the total number of Athenians was about 100-125,000 souls.

— What about the rest of the 400,000?

— Of the rest, around 30-50,000 people were *metics*, namely foreigners without any political rights, who worked in Athens having immigrated from other cities. These were the driving force of the Athenian economy. However, the majority of the population were *slaves*, usually war prisoners, charged with all sorts of daily tasks, offering citizens spare time to engage in private and mainly public affairs.

ANCIENT AGORA

— So, when we talk about ancient Athens, we refer chiefly to the asty. What was it like?

— The *asty* had developed on the flatland around the soaring Acropolis that dominated the landscape and served as the city's religious centre and symbol. However, the heart of the city beat in the Agora, situated at a lower level. It was an open space, surrounded by many public buildings and sanctuaries. Aside from its commercial character, the site was the centre of everyday political and social life. Merchants, pedlars, farmers, stockbreeders and fishermen hawked their goods, whereas groups of people walked among them and commented on anything that aroused their interest. In trading, they used the city's official coins and, in many cases, bartering —the exchange of goods without money— was practiced. For instance, they bartered eggs for pottery. Here, you could see everyone: from Socrates and his students, to the humblest slave bargaining over the price of fish, which the fishmonger had just brought from Halimous (present-day Alimos).

SPACES FOR MUSIC AND THEATRE

— On the other side of the Acropolis, on the south slope, lay the buildings where theatrical and music events were staged as part of the city's great festivals, the Dionysia and the Panathenaea: These were the Theatre of Dionysus (1), the Odeon of Pericles (2) and the Odeon of Herodes Atticus, widely known as Herodeion (3). All these buildings found together in this part of the city designated the area as the first cultural centre in history.

— Okay. Tell me a few words about each building!

— The Theatre of Dionysus is located within the precinct of the god's sanctuary, where the first theatrical performances in history were held already since the late 6th c. BC. Chronologically, the surviving theatre today is the third one, built in the 4th c. BC, and had a capacity of around 17,000 spectators. So, imagine the thousands of Athenians coming early in the morning from all parts of the city to grab their seats and watch tragedies and comedies being uninterruptedly performed, one after the other, all day long! After all, there were not any lamps and spotlights!

— What about the Odeon of Pericles?

— This building was possibly designed by Ictinus, the architect who built the Parthenon. It was not intended for music teaching as the word denotes today, but for concerts and musical contests organized during the Panathenaea festival. In fact, this building blazed a trail, as it was the first closed structure for concerts in the history of civilization. The first Music Hall, so to speak!!

— What did it look like?

— It was almost square in plan, around 3,500 square metres in area, featuring pyramidal roof supported by wooden pillars. In the centre, there was a platform on which musicians and singers stood, whereas 5,000 spectators would sit around on tiered wooden benches. What was interesting about this building was the fact that its pillars were originally the masts of the Persian ships wrecked during the Battle of Salamis, washed up on the shore of the Phaleric Bay! The Athenians kept them, and when they needed them 40 years later, they used them.

— So, the ancients actually knew how to recycle!

— They did a lot better than us! Nothing was cast away! They did not even have any garbage.

OTHER GREAT MONUMENTS

— We're a bit off course here, I think! From splendour to waste! Tell me about the Herodeion, where my parents frequently go; I just want to check whether they do know the monument's history!

— The Odeon of Herodes Atticus was built 600 years later to replace the Odeon of Pericles that lay in ruins! It was donated to the city around 160 AD by Herodes Atticus, an immensely rich sophist from Marathon, in memory of his wife Regilla. It had a seating capacity of about 6,000 spectators. Today, its roof is no longer preserved, but in Antiquity, its construction made use of ground-breaking technology, as it lacked columns supporting it internally, to ensure the unobstructed viewing of the plays. Edgy; don't you think?

— It sure was. Now talk to me about the rest of the city

— There were numerous sanctuaries and temples in other parts of the city as well, the most impressive of which was the temple of Olympian Zeus. Its construction began in the 6th century BC and, after many intervals in which work was suspended, it was eventually completed in the 2nd century AD. However, the best-preserved ancient temple in Greece is the one dedicated to Hephaestus, widely known today as the Theseion (Temple of Theseus).

— *Really? Why did its name change?*

— The name Theseion had been assigned in the past by the Athenians, because in one of its south metopes is depicted the fight between Theseus and the Minotaur. Later, archaeologists established the building's true identity. Between these great works stretched residential areas, occupied by the private residences of the Athenians, estimated at around 10,000. They were built next to winding streets, arranged in larger or smaller neighbourhoods, resembling present-day Plaka.

YOU
ARE
HERE

THE CITY'S FORTIFICATION WALL

— I think I have heard about the Themistoclean Wall. I gather from its name that it was a work by Themistocles. Ah! There he is. Let's invite him to talk to us about his ... wall.

THEMISTOCLES: Oh dear! You sure stirred up old memories, my friends! It was 479 BC; we had just ejected the Persians from Greece, and Athens had become stronger after the war. I knew that the Spartans and the city's other enemies would not be pleased with it. So, I thought we should defend our city by building a large and robust wall that would enclose the *asty*. I easily talked the Athenians into it, and we hastily built the wall within a year! We used every stone available, even from the graves of our ancestors which the Persians had destroyed. We all worked together from dawn to dusk. Can you imagine?

— How big was the wall you built, my general?

The wall's perimeter was 6.5 km, and it took more than two hours to walk along its outer circumference, following a road that surrounded the enclosure. Fifteen gates were arranged at intervals.

— Why so many?

Because, from these gates passed the roads that led to the *demes* but also areas outside Attica. Gradually, the wall demarcated the activities of citizens: Within the wall lay temples, sanctuaries, public spaces and dwellings, while outside the gates, along these roads, were established cemeteries, as well as workshops and artisanal installations.

THE KERAMEIKOS: AN ATHENIAN NEIGHBOURHOOD

— To get an idea of what the city looked like, come and see together from above a picture of west Athens.

— Oh, that's splendid! Please, show me!

— The ancient name of the area was Inner Kerameikos, found within the city's fortification wall. In the foreground we see the residential area that consisted of single-storey houses extending to the Themistoclean Wall. Dwellings did not feature any openings in their exterior walls, so that their residents could isolate themselves from the prying eyes of passers-by, but in the centre there was an inner courtyard where most of the household tasks took place. The centre of the picture is dominated by a large public building, called Pompeion that served as the starting point of religious processions, such as the Panathenaic procession. Two gates are visible next to it, the Sacred Gate to the left and the Dipylon Gate to the right. From the first gate passed the road that

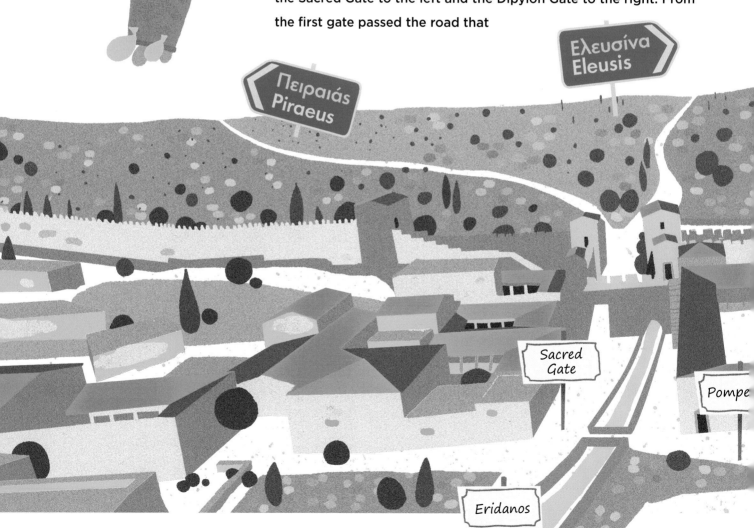

ended in Piraeus, and the Sacred Way (*Hiera Odos*) which connected Athens with Eleusis and, by extension, the Peloponnese and the rest of Greece. The road outside the second gate that led to the Academy was the public Cemetery (*Demosion Sema*) —a wide road on the sides of which the graves of those who died in battle and the city's illustrious figures were arranged. This is where the Athenian people gathered to listen to Pericles delivering his Funeral Oration (*Epitaph*) in 430 BC, occasioned by the burial of those who lost their lives first in the Peloponnesian War. This area outside the wall was occupied by the cemetery of the Kerameikos.

— What about those demes that were farther away? Were they like small villages?

— Pretty much. In the remote *demes* lived mainly farmers and stockbreeders, but in many of them, depending on their location, the inhabitants were loggers, as in the mountains of Penteli and Parnitha, miners as in Lavrion, but also fishermen as in the coastal *demes*.

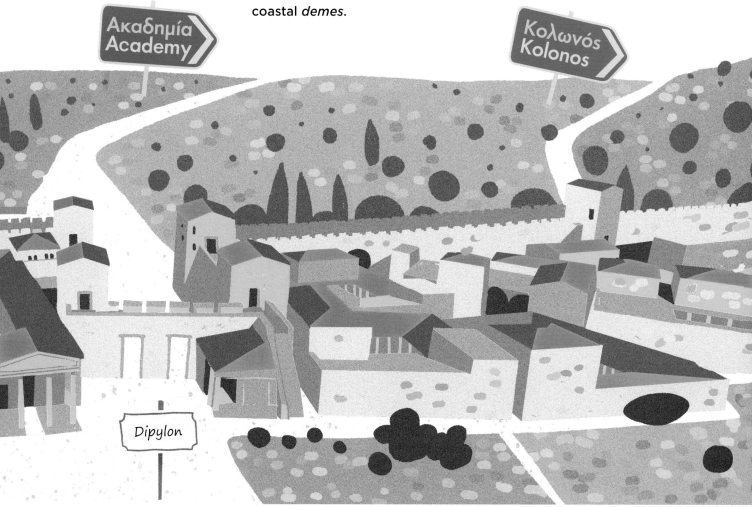

PIRAEUS

— Which was the most important deme?

— It was Piraeus, without a doubt. From the early 5th c. BC, it turned —once again on the initiative of Themistocles— into the city's most important commercial and military port, replacing Phaleron. Five stoae had been built at Piraeus intended for trading activities, whereas in its houses lived many merchants, mariners, migrants and people of the sea.

— I guess the port was always bustling!!

— Yes, it was! It had its own special fortification for its protection but, at the same time, it was connected to Athens through the Long Walls that ensured the circulation of people and the transport of goods to and from the sea, even in case of siege. Everything was shrewdly organized to serve the needs of the Athenians and their productive activities, but also to defend people when wars broke out, a frequent phenomenon back then.

— Where was the military harbour exactly?

— The Athenian navy was based in two smaller harbours of Piraeus, Zea (Pasalimani) and Munychia (Mikrolimano). They were equipped with special shipyards where 350 triremes were berthed in winter. Occasionally, in the harbour of Zea were moored ships that carried crops to the city; hence the name of the harbour, according to a view (Zea is a plant genus, widely known as maize).

ATHENS AND ATHENA

— Do you have any idea why the two names, of the city and the goddess Athena (Αθήνα), are very much alike? Is it true that the city was named after the goddess?

— It is just one letter that makes all the difference between the name of the city and that of the goddess! Impressive, isn't it? The word ATHENS (ΑΘΗΝΆ) is pre-Hellenic, befitting the city's prehistoric past; however, it is not easy to establish whether it was the city that was named after the goddess, as mythology has taught us, or it was the other way round. Nevertheless, we are almost certain that Athens was the first name of the Acropolis occupied by the prehistoric inhabitants. Later, the name included the lower city that developed around the rock.

ΑΘΗΝΆ

THE ACROPOLIS: THE CITY'S LANDMARK

— Having said all that, let's talk about the Acropolis. Why is it so important?

— To make this clear to you, let's start at the beginning: The Acropolis is a rock that became a fortress and seat of the region's rulers as early as 3200 BC. Its prominent location that ensured visual control of the surrounding area all the way to the sea, the relatively smooth terrain to build houses on, and the naturally fortified site which later, during the Mycenaean period, was reinforced with a cyclopean wall, were natural attributes that fulfilled the needs of people of the time. In addition, the natural springs on its slopes, but also the fertile, arable land of the neighbouring plain were significant advantages.

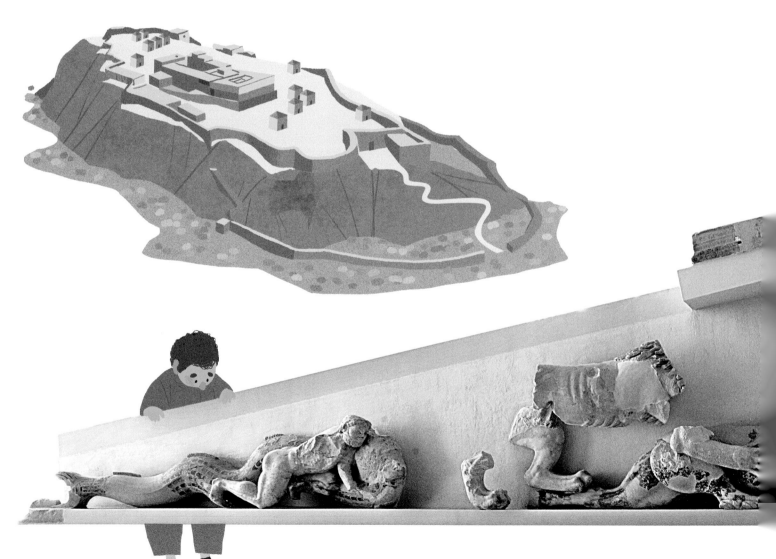

— I see; but how was it converted from a fortress into a sanctuary?

— Look! Modest places of worship existed on the rock from the start, located either outdoors or inside the Mycenaean palace. The Acropolis turned into the main sanctuary of Attica in the 8th c. BC when the city-state of Athens was established; as a result, in the Archaic period (7th–6th c. BC), houses gradually disappeared and religious activity increased.

— Do we know what the Acropolis looked like at that time?

— Yes, we do, quite well actually. Back then, in the time of the poet Solon and the tyrant Peisistratus, two large temples were built, where the cult of Athena was practiced, and 5–6 smaller ones were dedicated to other deities and local heroes. The temples were adorned with impressive sculptures depicting lions devouring other animals but also representations of gods, such as Zeus, or Heracles engaging in his early Labours. You can see all this in the Acropolis Museum. Shortly later, in 520–500 BC, the magnificent figure of Athena, shown pursuing the Giants (*Gigantes*) and defending the city, dominated one of the pediments.

POLYCHROME ARCHAIC KORAI

— Ah!!! There she is! She is so impressive, spreading her serpent-fringed aegis. But, what are these large marble statues displayed at the Museum?

— You mean the Korai! These are statues of maidens mainly, featuring imposing bodies, rich garments and restrained smile. More than 200 of them have been recovered on the Acropolis, either intact or in fragmentary condition. They were expensive works, usually dedicated by parents to put their children under the protection of the goddess, as they were mounted next to the temples and the altars of the sanctuary. Concurrently, through these votive offerings, families showed off their wealth and power to the entire city.

— How were the Korai statues made?

— At first, the sculptor who received the commission observed the maiden (1) and created a clay or plaster model roughly depicting the girl's outer appearance, but not her exact personal features as in a portrait. He then produced a copy, carved out of white marble and, finally, he applied colour to her garments, hair, pupils, lips and jewellery (2), thereby imparting liveliness and expression to his creation.

— What happened to the colours?

— They faded in the course of time as the statues were buried in the ground, so when they were unearthed during excavation, they gave the impression that they were totally white (3). However, modern technology enables us to reconstruct the actual colours and apply them to plaster casts (2) restoring the original form of the statues which were quite close to reality.

1

2

3

THE BIRTH OF DEMOCRACY

— All these things we have learned about the establishment of Democracy, did they occur at that time?

— Yes. At the end of the Archaic period, in 508 BC, a major event took place in Athens that changed the course of history: Until then, power was in the hands of the aristocrats who were usually in conflict with each other, unconcerned about the fate of ordinary people. After the expulsion of the sons of the tyrant Peisistratus, Cleisthenes, the new leader of the aristocrats, turned to the lower class of Athens in order to secure his position by granting people political rights for the first time. In addition, he established the

Pnyx, an open-air meeting place next to the Hill of the Muses, widely known today as Philopappos Hill, where the Athenian citizens gathered to listen to their leaders and vote for or against their proposals by show of hands.
This is how Democracy was born.

— Was it that simple?

— Today, it may look simple to us, but back then it was something exceptionally daring and ground-breaking! The new political system empowered everyone, even poor citizens, to participate in public affairs, depending on their social class. This infused the population, leaders and the people, with self-confidence and pride and inspired them to create. Simultaneously, the Athenians took measures to protect the new system against threats. Therefore, they introduced ostracism, a process in which people chose by voting to banish anyone powerful that was likely to put Democracy in danger. They used potsherds as voting tokens, inscribed with the name and the patronym of the nominated person.

— Why didn't they use paper?

— Paper, as we know it today, did not exist at that time. Papyrus, which was imported from Egypt, was rare and very expensive.

Finally, in the 4th c. BC, a time when the political system was once again endangered, they enacted a law, according to which anyone who decided to kill an aspirant tyrant would avoid prosecution. This decision was inscribed on a marble stele still preserved today at the Stoa of Attalos.

THE ACROPOLIS DURING THE PERSIAN WARS

— I presume you remember from history the Persian Wars and the great battles which the Greeks fought to thwart the enemy.

— Yes! I remember quite well that initially, in the first invasion in 490 BC, the Athenians defeated them at Marathon, owing to Miltiades's military genius.

— That's right! What you may not know though is the self-sacrifice of the polemarch Kallimachos who in the end died heroically in this battle. For his deed, right after the battle, the Athenians dedicated at the Acropolis a marble statue of flying Nike, who spread the message of victory across the city, standing on a tall Ionic column. You can see the 5-metre-high monument at the Acropolis Museum, where it is on display, and you can recall the Battle of Marathon and Kallimachos's bravery. Besides, this is the role of monuments: they remind us of great events that we sometimes tend to forget.

— I have heard though that the Persians destroyed Athens and the Acropolis.

— Yes. This happened during the second invasion in 480 BC. Following their victory at Thermopylae, the Persian forces reached Athens where they besieged the Acropolis and burned it. Then, all of its temples were set on fire, while the Archaic statues and other votive offerings found among the fire debris were shattered.

— What happened to the Athenians?

— The Athenians who fled to Salamis, but even those who were on the warships could see the Acropolis and their city in flames and lamented their land, pondering their bleak future in anguish. Nevertheless, they hadn't said their last word. Not too long afterwards, in the naval battle that took place right in front of them, in the straits of Salamis, the strategic acumen of Themistocles led the united Greeks to victory, by crushing the Persian fleet and expelling the enemy from Athens.

— Did the Athenians return after the victory?

— Yes! They returned to find their homes and sanctuaries made into a heap of burnt ruins. Yet, they were not disheartened. The fact that they had overpowered a mightier enemy encouraged them to rebuild their city. But try to see this differently: The destruction of the Acropolis by the Persians, although it was painful, in the end yielded a positive outcome! Because, if the Persians had not destroyed the Archaic temples, the Athenians would never have built new ones, at least in the Classical period.

THE ACROPOLIS OF THE CLASSICAL PERIOD

— It would never cross my mind that a disaster could actually work out for the best! How were all these works we see created?

— Around 450 BC, thirty years after the Persian wars, the Athenian state launched a major building programme centred on the Acropolis. The programme was devised by Pericles himself and his political and artistic team. When they were ready, Pericles addressed the Athenians in the *Ekklesia tou Demou* (Assembly) and presented the programme delivering a fiery speech. Can you imagine this unique meeting at the Pnyx?

— I am trying to! I guess, the Athenians approved it immediately!

— No, it was not that easy! Pericles utilized his rhetorical skill, arguing that the city would become so beautiful that all Athenians would be proud of it. Furthermore, he added that in this great public undertaking everyone would be able to find a job, because unemployment was high at that time. Therefore, he convinced them to vote for the construction of three temples dedicated to the goddess Athena, that would replace those destroyed by the Persians.

— Why three and not just one?

— Because each temple would serve the different roles of the goddess: the Parthenon (1) would be dedicated to Athena Parthenos, namely young Athena in her capacity as a goddess of war. For Athena Polias (the city's patron goddess) they would build the Erectheion (2), and finally for Athena, as a goddess of victory in times of war, they would erect the temple of Athena Nike (3). In addition to the temples, they decided to create a monumental propylon (4) that would receive visitors to the Acropolis and prepare them for the splendid monuments they would encounter once they entered.

THE BUILDING PROGRAMME OF PERICLES

— Were all these buildings constructed concomitantly?

— By and large, yes. They were all built within a period of 40 years, yet gradually, one after the other, depending on each year's means and planning. The first works, the Parthenon and the Propylaea, were built in a relatively short time, and Pericles was fortunate enough to inaugurate them himself. The Erechtheion and the temple of Athena Nike were constructed during the Peloponnesian War (431–404 BC) which, as you remember, was fought between Athens and Sparta and ended in the crushing defeat of Athens. However, all these monuments endured and justified the choices of Pericles and the Athenian people.

— So, what purpose did the Acropolis works serve?

— The building programme of Pericles served many purposes: To begin with, the new temples expressed the gratitude of the Athenians to the gods for their assistance in the victories over the Persians. Furthermore, the entire area was restored and rearranged, while the sanctuary was enhanced so as to receive worshippers, every time the Panathenaea festival was celebrated. Finally, the magnificence of the new buildings and their sculptural decoration highlighted the significance of the city and asserted its intention to become Greece's new leading power. Because, until then, no one could dispute the dominance of Sparta.

— How were these works financed? I suppose they must have cost huge amounts of money.

— That's true! It has been estimated that in today's terms they cost more than one billion euros. The money came mainly from the Persian spoils and the proceeds of the sanctuary. It is not true that their construction was funded through the tribute paid by the allies of Athens, since only 1/60 of it ended up in the treasury of the goddess.

— Tell me a few more things about Pericles!

— If that's alright with you, let's invite him to talk to us about himself.

PERICLES: Well, my children, I was born in 495 BC into the noble family of the Alcmaeonidae. My father was Xanthippos and my mother was Agariste. After completing my studies under the best tutors, I soon engaged in public affairs, like all young aristocrats of the time, and in 461 BC I became leader of the democratic party. Since then, and for 32 consecutive years (461–429 BC), I was elected *strategos* (military leader), I governed the Athenian state, and I feel proud that I succeeded, like nobody else, in giving prominence to my city as a military, political and artistic centre. In fact, I dare say that I am happy, because history has honoured me by naming one of the most glorious eras, the so-called "golden age", after me.

PROPYLAEA: THE GREAT ENTRANCE

— What exactly is the Propylaea?

— The Propylaea is an impressive entryway. Although it featured large colonnades and triangular pediments, it was not a temple. As a matter of fact, the building had 5 gates; hence, the word in Greek is in the plural: Propylaea.

— Five gates? Imagine the swarm of people going in and out!

— Not all gates were open, except for the period of the great festivals, such as the Panathenaea, when all Athenians ascended the Acropolis. The rest of the time, only the left gate remained open, as evidenced by the greater wear on its threshold.

— Tell me about the building's architecture.

— Its construction was launched in 437 BC, following the completion of the Parthenon, based on the designs by the architect Mnesicles. Judging by the many similarities to the great temple, such as the coexistence of Ionic and Doric columns, we may assume that Mnesicles was a student of Ictinus and that the two structures were most likely built by the same construction crew.

— What exactly did Mnesicles accomplish?

— His major accomplishment was that he imparted to an entrance building the form and splendour of a great temple. The originality of the design lies in the fact that for the first time a building opened up like an imaginary embrace to welcome visitors.

Pinakothe

— What was the Pinakotheke people talk about? Was it an art gallery, like today?

— Not exactly! It was a reception hall, with 17 couches around the walls, situated to the left of the Propylaea entry point, where banquets (*symposia*) were held for the official visitors during the religious festivals celebrated on the Acropolis. To create a pleasant atmosphere, the walls of this chamber were decorated with paintings (*pinakes*) depicting mythological scenes, such as the feats of Odysseus, Diomedes and Orestes! This is why the chamber was called *Pinakotheke*.

TEMPLE OF ATHENA OR APTEROS (WINGLESS) NIKE

— As we have said, one of the roles in which Athena was worshipped on the sacred rock was that of Nike (Victory). The Athenians built the temple during the Peloponnesian War, in a difficult period when they desperately needed the assistance of their goddess. Simultaneously, in order to highlight some of their military victories, they adorned the frieze of the temple with scenes from their triumphant battles.

— *Why is the building also called temple of Apteros (Wingless) Nike?*

— This name is ancient, but is the result of a misunderstanding. The temple was not dedicated to Nike but to Athena, whose cult statue naturally did not have any wings. However, during the

Roman period, when the building was commonly known as temple of Nike, the absence of wings on the statue was erroneously ascribed to their removal by the Athenians, so that Nike (Victory) would never leave their city!

— Its architectural form seems somewhat unusual. Am I right?

— You are absolutely right! It features only four columns on the main facade and the back. These columns, 4 m in height, are monolithic, which means that they were made of a single stone block, bearing close resemblance to the Ionic columns of the Propylaea, although they are only half their size.

— I see it is studded with sculptures! Why so many?

Indeed! They are many because, aside from the pediments and the frieze, the roof was surmounted by 6 gilt-bronze acroteria, all depicting the flying figure of Nike! Can you imagine how they would shine under the sunlight?

— There are also reliefs around the temple.

— That's true! They formed part of the relief parapet, namely a low wall with a metal railing on top, surrounding the courtyard to protect the faithful who gathered around the temple from falling off the rock. The parapet was embellished with about 50 relief winged Nikai preparing a sacrifice to Athena.

— Wow! All these reliefs are so beautiful!!!

— You're right! Even nowadays, we are enraptured by the young female figures with the exceptional movement, the solidly built bodies and the transparent garments. The most famous of all is the Nike shown lifting her leg to take off her sandal and climb to the altar barefoot for the sacrifice. With a human, everyday motion, the figure becomes lively, enabling the sculptor to highlight the beauty of her body and, at the same time, his own unparalleled artistic skill.

ERECHTHEION: THE ARC OF MYTHS

— The Erechtheion looks rather strange for a temple. Why was it important to the Athenians?

— This temple was also dedicated to Athena and, in fact, it was the most sacred temple on the Acropolis, because the most ancient statue of the goddess was kept there, made of olive wood, which, according to tradition, had fallen from the sky!

— Okay! Did the ancients actually believe such things? And if it was a temple dedicated to Athena, why was it called Erechtheion?

— It was called Erechtheion during the Roman period. Originally, it was called temple of Athena Polias. It is built on the site of the Mycenaean megaron, where perhaps Athena was initially worshipped by Erechtheus who was a Mycenaean king.

— Any way! Its architecture is quite curious.

— Indeed! It is not characterized by the symmetry and regularity typically found in ancient temples. It is a complex structure in which the architect —probably Mnesicles who had also built the Propylaea— succeeded in combining heterogeneous elements into a single form in order to create one of the most refined and elegant works of ancient Greek architecture.

— You didn't answer my question though, why all these peculiarities?

— The special character of the Erechtheion derives from the fact that it was not only the cult of Athena practiced in its premises, but also the cults of other Olympian gods, such as Poseidon and Zeus. In addition, the building housed the marks of their divine presence on the rock which, according to the Athenian tradition, had been formed during the contest between Athena and Poseidon over the city's patronage, when Athena brought forth an olive tree, Poseidon produced water with his trident, and Zeus ended their rivalry by hurling the thunderbolt. Furthermore, beneath the building lay the tombs of earlier kings and heroes, founders of the city, such as Erechtheus and Cecrops. In fact, the Karyatids stand above these tombs, guarding and honouring the sacred relics of the Acropolis, since the Erechtheion served as the arc of all of the city's myths and traditions.

PARTHENON: THE MOST MAGNIFICENT TEMPLE

— We have finally reached the Parthenon! Please, explain to me, why is this temple the most significant of all?

— It is true that the Parthenon, the temple of Athena Parthenos, is the most important ancient Greek temple, for its architectural perfection, its sculptural decoration and also for the symbolisms it emanated concerning the power and radiance of the city. Moreover, it is significant because it was built at a time when the political system of Athens was Democracy, and the city had visionary leaders, proud and safe citizens and, of course, abundant financial resources. All these, in conjunction with the collaboration of inspired creators and outstanding craftsmen, led to this great achievement.

— Who were responsible for its construction?

— The architects of the temple, Ictinus and Callicrates, were commissioned following a competition, whereas the project was supervised by Pericles's friend, the sculptor Pheidias, who undertook the creation of the chryselephantine statue of Athena that would be housed in the new temple. These people were in charge of the works. However, responsible for the financial management were the *epistates* (overseers), namely public officials appointed for one year, accountable to the *Ekklesia tou Demou* (Assembly), the Athenian people.

— What did the duties of the epistates involve?

— In accordance with the specifications, they purchased materials, paid daily wages and covered all expenses. At the end of their term, they handed over the treasury to their successors documenting in marble stelae the works and their cost, as well as the amount of money still available. The stelae were mounted on the Acropolis next to the monuments, so that anyone could inspect the sound management of public funds.

— Ah, I see! This is called transparency! What else do these inscriptions tell us?

— They tell us a lot. As each year's stele was dated, they inform us about the progress of the works. For instance, we know that construction work of the Parthenon began in 448–447 BC when the first marble blocks were cut in the quarry of Mount Penteli, and that the building was completed within 10 years, whereas by 432 BC, the entire sculptural decoration had been affixed.

THE PARTHENON'S WORKSITE

— So, there was a proper worksite on the rock with labourers and craftsmen, wasn't there?

— There were many worksites. The works on the Acropolis constituted a major public undertaking that, as Pericles had promised, gave work to many people. These people worked throughout the week, from dawn to dusk as quarrymen at Penteli, as carriers of marble and other materials and, the majority of them, as stone carvers, because stone blocks were treated by hand, using hammers and chisels on the Acropolis rock, in front of the monuments. Of course, the final polishing of the walls and the columns was performed only after they had been mounted at their exact position on the monument, with the aid of high-precision wooden cranes. In addition, there were many more specialties, such as sculptors, painters, ropemakers, carpenters, but also specialized craftsmen who made and repaired devices and tools. There must have been a patchwork of people working there, but surely there was excellent organization, coordination and collaboration between them.

— Now, answer me something else: Were all these workers freemen or slaves?

— An inscription at the Erechtheion (right), in which the remuneration paid to stone carvers and sculptors in 408/7 BC is recorded, gives us an idea of the kind of people who worked on the Acropolis. From the inscription it transpires that only 30% were Athenian citizens, while 50% were metics and 20% were slaves.

List of artists and craftsmen

45

MEN AND ANIMALS AT WORK

— Thank you! How was the heavy marble transferred from Penteli to the Acropolis really?

— As we have said, marble was extracted from the quarries of Mount Penteli in the form of unprocessed blocks, whose weight was much heavier that the final one. These blocks were loaded onto special wooden platforms (called *chelonai* in Greek, namely tortoises), which were taken down from the mountain by means of rollers underneath. On flat terrain, marble blocks were moved to very strong carts pulled by many oxen or mules together.

— I would imagine though that in upward slopes things were much tougher!

— Indeed! However, the ancients, who were practical people, devised various clever solutions about everything. For instance, in order to elevate to the Acropolis a massive column capital from the steep slope in front of the Propylaea, they did the following: Instead of using the oxen to draw the heavy cart uphill, they fastened a very long and strong rope to the cart that was then passed around a firmly fixed rock on the hilltop, allowing the animals to easily pull the cart upwards while they were moving downwards, as shown on the picture.

— Oh dear!! These poor animals must have suffered so much!

— Aristotle actually recounts a very interesting story about one of them.

— Please, tell me about it!!

— There was once a mule which had worked for many years carrying and moving marble blocks from Penteli to the Parthenon. When it grew old, the Athenians decided to relieve the animal from its services and even to feed it for free. Nevertheless, it had become so accustomed to the itinerary that, every morning, it joined the rest of the animals from the Kerameikos to Penteli and returned with them to Athens, of course without carrying anything on its back!!

PARTHENON: ARCHITECTURAL FEATURES

— Talk to me about the architecture of the Parthenon.
How is it different from the other temples?

— The Parthenon is a peipteral Doric temple with 8 columns on its narrow sides and 17 on its long sides; hence, it is surrounded by a total of 46 columns. In addition, at the front and rear faces of the cella, namely the central part of the building, it features a pronaos and an opisthodomos respectively, that each one had 6 columns. So, to the 46 columns you should add 12 more. Are you counting?

— I am; let's move on! What was it like inside.
Were there any other columns?

— The cella was divided into two unequal parts. The largest one, where the chryselephantine statue of Athena was housed, featured a Pi-shaped colonnade consisting of 23 columns. Given that this was a two-storey colonnade, you should add 46 more columns to those of the temple's exterior. Furthermore, the west compartment of the cella that contained the city's treasury (something like a present-day central bank) was supported by 4 soaring Ionic columns. This means that the Parthenon had a total of 108 columns! Can you believe this?

— Yes, but I could not possibly imagine that it also served as a treasury …

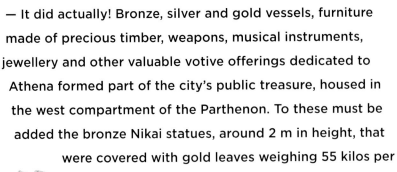

— It did actually! Bronze, silver and gold vessels, furniture made of precious timber, weapons, musical instruments, jewellery and other valuable votive offerings dedicated to Athena formed part of the city's public treasure, housed in the west compartment of the Parthenon. To these must be added the bronze Nikai statues, around 2 m in height, that were covered with gold leaves weighing 55 kilos per statue. So, whenever the city needed money, they could remove parts of this gold to mint coins.

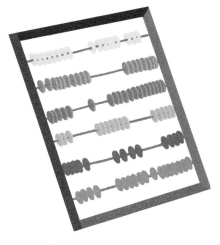

46 on the peristasis
6 + 6 = 12 on the prostaseis
23 + 23 = 46 in the interior
4 west compartment
= 108 columns

In the same space were also kept the tributes of the allied city-states of the Delian League.

— *Wow!!*

— Do you want me to go on with its architecture? The Parthenon is one of the largest classical temples. It is 69.50 m long and 30.88 m wide; hence, it occupies an area of more than 2,000 square metres, half the size of a football court! It is built of 16,500 marble members of varying size, such as massive architraves, 4.30 m in length and 5–10 tons in weight, whereas its roof was covered by 9,000 marble tiles. Do you want me to say more?

— *No more figures! Please!!! Let's take a look at its form. Despite its size, it does not seem bulky, but harmonious.*

OPTICAL REFINEMENTS AND OTHER ... RIDDLES

— Indeed! The Parthenon is marked by two more special features: one of the them is its *eumetria*, namely its good measure, as you've already noticed yourself. There is a balanced and harmonious relationship between the building's three dimensions, but also between many of its individual elements. The other feature, which I guess is not easily noticeable at first glance, is the temple's optical *refinements*, these subtle and imperceptible deviations from regularity.

— *Refinements! Such a nice word! How do we see them?*

— Optical refinements are noticed mainly on the building's horizontal surfaces, forming indiscernible curves, but also on its vertical elements (walls and columns) that deviate from their axis. Hence, none of the monument's lines are perfectly straight and none of its surfaces are perfectly flat. However, the most impressive quality is that these characteristics are not immediately visible, but call for the observer's attention and concentration. You don't usually see them, unless a guide points them out to you!

— *Why did the ancients do all that? Let me guess: They wanted to be original! They wanted to do something no one else had done before!*

— This may be true! However, their main intention, through these special shapes and volumes, was purely aesthetic.

— What do you mean?

— Look! They built this great edifice in such a way so as to invest it with elegance and grace. In addition, they succeeded in giving life and movement, divesting it of stiffness and rigidity. And the most fascinating of all is that we practically cannot see this! Through these refinements, the building was infused with inner harmony, creating a secret connective tissue spread across the entire structure, even its innermost parts!

— This is not very clear to me, but if you show me some details and examples, I might be able to understand what you mean.

— Instead of tiresome examples, I prefer that we take a look at this deliberately exaggerated drawing of the temple, so that we can instantly understand the form of these refinements.

— Okay!

— Let's start from the temple's stylobate, namely the surface upon which the columns rest. The stylobate is not flat, but curves, forming an upward bulge. The same occurs in all other horizontal parts of the temple, even on higher levels, up to the roof! Impressive; Isn't it?

— It is, indeed!

— Now, if we take a closer look at the columns, we will find out they are not proper cylinders, but taper towards the top. Moreover, they are not perpendicular to the stylobate, but lean slightly inwards, whereas a similar inclination is observed on the walls of the cella. I know, I have tired you out, but I am not over yet! The distances between the columns are not equal, but those columns near the corners are more densely arranged as opposed to the central ones, which are more sparsely placed.

— Enough! I know now why the Parthenon is a unique monument.

PARTHENON: THE SCULPTURAL DECORATION

— So far, we have only talked about architecture! Wait till you see the temple's sculptures.

— Go on!

— In terms of quantity, quality and content, the sculptural decoration of the Parthenon measures up to its architecture. Responsible for its design was Pheidias, but many sculptors collaborated for its execution including his best students. Although he was present from the commencement of the works and created, as we have already said, the chryselephantine statue of Athena, it seems that he only worked there until 438 BC, since he then moved to Olympia to construct the chryselephantine statue of Zeus.

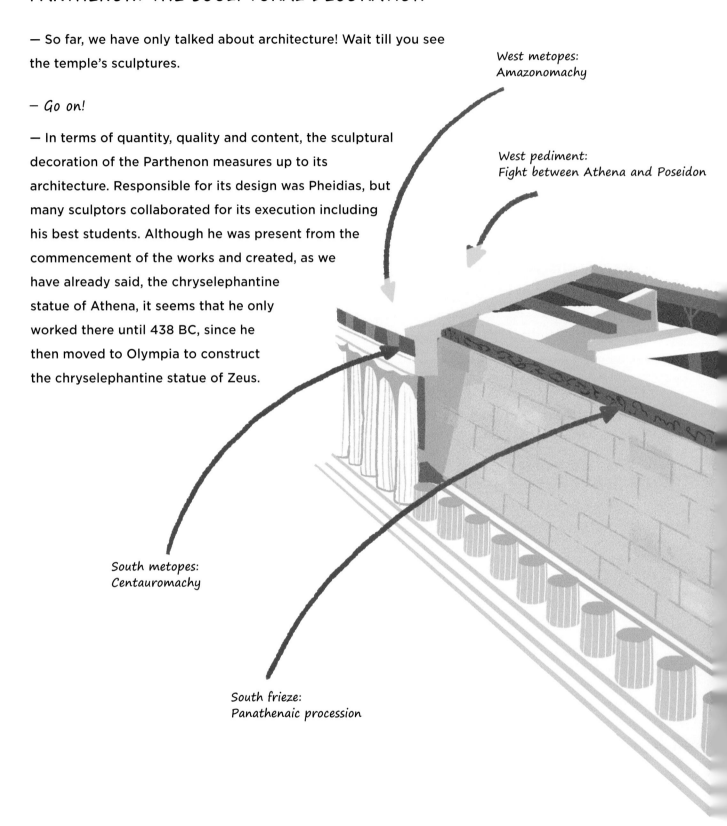

West metopes:
Amazonomachy

West pediment:
Fight between Athena and Poseidon

South metopes:
Centauromachy

South frieze:
Panathenaic procession

— So, he was in high demand! He couldn't get around to doing it all!

— It is true that Pheidias was considered the most suitable artist to depict the magnificence of the gods. Therefore, you can understand why he was greatly sought after. Even so, it could be argued that by designing the Parthenon's sculptural decoration, he pushed the envelope, since he decorated with sculptures the building's two pediments, 92 metopes and the entire frieze that was 160 m long!!

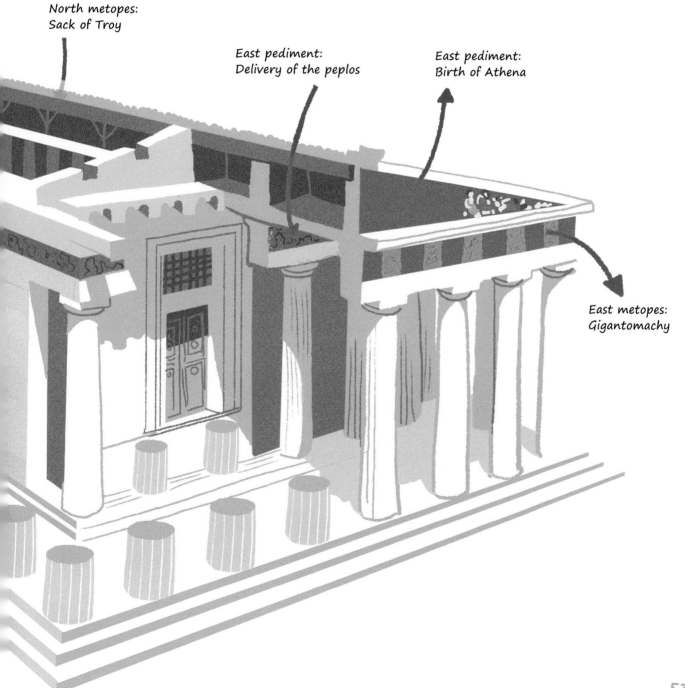

North metopes:
Sack of Troy

East pediment:
Delivery of the peplos

East pediment:
Birth of Athena

East metopes:
Gigantomachy

THE SCULPTURES AT THE MUSEUM

— Ah! The Parthenon Gallery at the Museum is truly wonderful.

— Yes, it is! The exhibition of the Parthenon sculptures at the Acropolis Museum is unique, as it combines authentic marble works, or parts of them, with plaster casts of those held in other museums abroad, mainly the British Museum, where they ended up following their seizure by Lord Elgin in 1801–1803. Hence, visitors can enjoy the overall form of the works in a gallery that has the same dimensions and orientation as the temple.

— Look! From this side we can see the monument on the rock!

— Yes! The Museum's direct visual contact with the temple turns the visit into a genuine experience. It is as though the building is notionally reunited with its sculptural decoration.

THE METOPES OF THE BATTLES

— First things first. Where do we start?

— We will start with the metopes found above the exterior columns surrounding the temple. As we have already stressed, the fact that all 92 metopes have been decorated, in contrast to other temples in which only the facade metopes were adorned, is unprecedented. On each side of the temple unfolds the narrative of a conflict from the mythical past: On the east side, above the temple's entrance, was depicted the struggle between the gods and the Giants (*Gigantomachy*); the west side was occupied by the battle of the Athenians with the Amazons (*Amazonomachy*); on the north side were illustrated scenes from the sack of Troy, and finally, the south side was dedicated to the Centauromachy.

The episodes of each narrative take the form of single combats pictured on each metope.

— What did these representations mean to the ancient Athenians?

— If you focus on the pairs of opponents in the metopes, on one side you will see the "bad guys", such as barbarians, foreigners, intruders, or claimants (Giants, Amazons, Centuars, Trojans), and on the other side are found the "good guys", namely gods, the Greeks, the Athenians, the civilized.

— It was all nicely set out by Pheidias!

— Yes, it was! What we see here is an artistic symbolism of the eternal battle between the forces of light and civilization and those of darkness and brutality.

— Are my eyes deceiving me? Most of the metopes have been damaged!

— Yes!! The figures in the metopes from the temple's three sides have been scraped off.

— Who did this?

— We do not know, but it must have happened in late Antiquity. It was either the barbarians who invaded Athens in AD 396, or fanatic Christians during the temple's conversion into a church.

THE FRIEZE OF PEACE

— What else are we going to see?

— The Parthenon frieze. It consists of 115 slabs; it is 160 m long, around 1 m high and encircles the top part of the exterior wall of the cella. Its subject differs from the rest of the sculptural decoration, as it depicts a real event that took place at that time: it was the Panathenaic procession, the city's "national" festival celebrated every four years in honour of the goddess Athena.

— What exactly was the Panathenaic procession?

— It was the most spectacular event of the Panathenaea festival. The procession started from the Kerameikos and ended in the Acropolis, in the altar of Athena next to the Erechtheion. It was held on the morning of the 28th day of the month Hekatombaion (mid-August). The entire Athenian population participated, men, women and children, even foreigners and slaves, because that day was a public holiday. Imagine a bustling crowd of older and younger people, locals and foreigners, jostling against each other, talking and gesturing as they followed the procession. The procession was led by priests, archons, foreign ambassadors and other officials, who accompanied the new peplos, the new garment that would replace the old one to adorn the goddess's old wooden statue at the Erechtheion.

— Why did they have to change the statue's garment every time?

— The renewal of the peplos every four years was an age-old magical ritual. The ancients believed that by replacing the old garment with a new one, the goddess and their city would be reanimated and reinforced. In fact, the peplos was woven by the *ergastinai*, young girls of Athenian aristocratic descent, a fact that gained their families prestige.

— How can we visualize the procession?

— We should think of the Panathenaic procession as a combination of a litany and a parade: It was a litany, since it was held in the context of a religious festival, its ritual rhythm was slow, and involved the transfer of sacred objects and offerings to the goddess. The parade was indicated by the "city's brilliant youths", the ephebes and the beautiful maidens carrying offerings in their hands, and also by the presence of the Athenian cavalry. These evoked a sense of pride among parents and fellow citizens, but at the same time, functioned as a way of demonstrating the Athenian power to allies and enemies.

HORSES, APOBATAI AND ... OIL

— Are all these things you have been talking about depicted on the frieze?

— More or less. The frieze constitutes a selective presentation of the procession. A total of 378 human figures and more than 220 animals —mostly horses— are depicted. On the west side of the temple, the one we encounter as we enter the Propylaea, are shown the procession's preparation and formation. Twenty-six riders, horses and people on foot are portrayed in various positions and movements, waiting to start marching.

— What happens next?

— On the two long sides, the north and the south, the procession is well underway, with a similar arrangement of the scenes. The narrative begins with 60 horsemen in different positions and postures. Around the centre unfold scenes of one of the most popular competitions of the Panathenaea, the *apobates* race.

— Apobates race? What's this?

— It was a very difficult competition, a kind of chariot race, in which young helmeted men, holding shield, known as *apobatai*, jumped off and on a moving chariot driven by a charioteer.

— Wow! It sounds difficult, but also impressive to watch. Was it performed during the procession?

— No! The athletic and equestrian events of the Panathenaea were conducted in the previous days, originally along the Panathenaic Way, in the section that passed through the city's Agora. Later, in the 4th c. BC, the competitions were held in the Panathenaic Stadium and the hippodrome.

— Did they stage any other events?

— Of course, they did!! They held musical events, including kithara, aulos and singing contests, as well as rhapsodic competitions in which the Homeric epics were recited. These events took place originally in the Agora, but from the mid-5th c. BC onwards they were staged at the Odeon of Pericles on the south slope of the Acropolis.

— What was the prize for the winners? Was it a plain wreath, as in Olympia?

— The wreath was among the rewards, but here the Athenians gave very rich prizes aiming to lay greater emphasis on their competitions. To the winners in music contests, they offered precious and highly expensive gold and silver wreaths, and to the winners in athletic and equestrian events, the prize involved large quantities of the sacred oil of Athena in clay vases, the so-called Panathenaic amphorae. However, the Panathenaea has distracted us from the monument. Let's go back to the frieze.

THE DELIVERY OF THE PEPLOS AND THE GODS

— What goes on at the east side of the frieze? I guess, it must be something important because it is found above the temple's main entrance.

— That's true! Here, we see the procession's arrival at its destination and the symbolic meeting of the two parties. In the centre is depicted the culminating moment of the celebration, which is the delivery of the new peplos to the priest of Athena. A child hands over to the priest the folded garment, while a priestess welcomes two maidens that carry cushioned seats on the heads. What is fascinating is that the sacred act takes place before the Olympian gods who seem carefree or talk to each other, divided into two groups. They are portrayed sitting on stools, with the exception of the enthroned Zeus —a possible indication that they are not on Mount Olympus but have temporarily come to the Acropolis to attend the cult rituals held in their honour. The fact that they turn their back to the procession suggests that the mortals cannot see them, as they are in their own world.

— Which gods do we see?

— From left, we see Hermes, Dionysus, Demeter, Ares, Hera (together with little Iris or Hebe) and Zeus. From right are shown Athena, Hephaestus, Poseidon talking with Apollo, Artemis touching Aphrodite's arm and little Eros.

Hermes   Dionysus   Demeter   Ares   Iris   Hera   Zeus

— How do we know who is who; they all look the same!

— Not quite so! Originally, each god carried his own symbol; for instance, Poseidon held a trident that is no longer preserved. Moreover, there are certain elements, such as their position, that betray their identity. Zeus and Athena, for example, are the central figures. Is this a coincidence? Certainly not! In addition, some figures, such as Apollo and Artemis, were always depicted side by side, because they were siblings.

Scene of delivering the peplos   Athena   Hephaestus   Poseidon   Apollo   Artemis   Aphrodite   Eros

MEN AND ANIMALS ON THE FRIEZE

— The faces of the gods are so beautiful and serene.

— Yes, they are! The entire frieze allows us to admire the faces of the figures. They are calm, full of gentleness, and are not disfigured by the intensity of the movements. They all seem concentrated on what they do but, at the same time, some gazes meet each other, unveiling a literal as well as metaphorical inwardness. The way they have been captured in one of the greatest moments in the history of art makes them look as though they are found in an ideal state.

— The animals are equally impressive, aren't they?

— Yes. On the three sides (west, north and south), horses equally participate with men, offering powerful moments, imparting vitality to the representation: Either with their intense and vigorous movements or with expressions of tenderness, when the riders caress them to calm them down. The rest of the animals, cows and rams, look restless, as if they have sensed their imminent sacrifice.

— Will you tell me a few more things about the sacrifice?

— Yes. The sacrifice of animals was the most important manifestation of every cult and took place at the end of festivals. Animals were sacrificed at the altar and then their meat was boiled or roasted and, finally, it was shared among the faithful, so that anyone could taste a portion of the now "divine" food. The Panathenaea sacrifice was a *hecatomb*, which means that one hundred oxen were sacrificed to Athena.

— Wow! Can you imagine the quantities of meat shared?

— It could feed the thousands of worshippers, who patiently waited for their turn. Bear in mind that for poorer people, a public sacrifice was the only chance they had to eat meat, since they could not afford to buy it for themselves!

— How often did such sacrifices occur?

— Very often! The Athenians were famous in antiquity for their piety.

— Or for their love of meat, perhaps?

THE DESIGN AND THE BEAUTY OF THE FRIEZE

— Okay! Enough with the blood and the meat; let's go back to the beauty of the frieze.

— You're right! Artistically, the frieze is an unparalleled work, marked by perfection in the rendering of the figures down to the smallest detail. There is a great variety and alternation of themes: people on foot, horsemen, chariots, animals. We also see the splendid overlap of figures against the relief's shallow depth. There are many other artistic tricks that give the work rhythm permeating the entire representation from one end to the other.

— Tell me, if you know, how was the frieze designed?

— Pheidias must have given serious thought to the work before creating this multifigure composition that conveys so many meanings. I am sure that he repeatedly shared his drawings and ideas with Ictinus, Pericles and Aspasia, but also with his students and collaborators. When he finally decided what to do, he must have calculated the cost, mainly the daily wages of the craftsmen and artists, which would have to be approved by the *Ekklesia tou Demou* (Assembly) in 442 BC, as was the case with all expenses of the undertaking.

— How were the reliefs carved?

— Look, since the stones of the frieze were actually building blocks and not slabs, their carving took place on site, in

contrast to the metopes and the pediments that were rendered in a workshop and mounted in place completed. So, I gather that once the 115 blocks were installed to form the 160-metre-long decorative zone, Pheidias climbed up the scaffolding, unfolded the papyrus with his preliminary drawings and started sketching the figures on the marble with charcoal. Then, simple stone carvers set to work using hammers and chisels to remove thick marble flakes around the figures, which gradually stood out from the background. This was followed by the next processing stages undertaken by sculptors who used more refined tools. Finally, the figures were polished with files and emery, and were coloured by painters, while complementary metal attachments were fixed, such as harnesses, weapons, vessels, symbols of the gods, etc.

— Wow!! I can only imagine the effort and the artistry to create this masterpiece!!

— Aside from the high art we behold, Pheidias resorted to many other clever solutions, such as isocephaly.

— What is this? It sounds like a disease!

— Isocephaly is the artistic canon according to which all figures, whether standing or seated, are at the same height. For instance, in the centre of the east frieze, the gods are depicted seated. If they stood up, they would be taller than the people standing next to them. In this way, their significance in the representation is further accentuated.

Helios   Dionysus   Persephone   Demeter   Eileithyia   Ares   Eros-Aphrodite   Hera   Iris   Zeus

EAST PEDIMENT

— We have finally reached the pediments!

— The two pediments constitute the culmination of the temple's sculptural decoration, since they occupy its highest part. Rendered between 437 and 432 BC, they depict mythological representations associated with the goddess Athena: On the east pediment, over the entrance, was depicted the miraculous birth of the goddess from the head of her father, Zeus. However, Athena is portrayed already fully grown and equal to her father. To their left and right, the rest of the gods are divided into two groups: Those who are nearer, have taken notice of the birth and behold the miracle ecstatically. The others, who have not realized yet what happened, remain isolated talking carelessly with each other.

thena   Hephaestus   Poseidon   Apollo   Artemis   Hermes   Hestia   Dione   Aphrodite   Selene

— Who are these gods? Can we identify them, like we did
on the frieze?

— Next to Zeus is depicted Hera, of course, together with Iris,
and next to Athena stands Hephaestus who, according to legend,
assisted in her birth by opening with his axe Zeus's head from
which Athena emerged. They were followed by other gods
either standing or sitting: To the right were Poseidon, Apollo,
Artemis and Hermes. To the left were Aphrodite, Ares, Demeter,
Persephone and Dionysus. Finally, in the two corners were
depicted Helios rising with his four-horse chariot on the left, and
Selene on the right sinking in the sea as she drives her chariot,
thereby indicating the time in which the events took place.

WEST PEDIMENT

— What have we got on the west pediment? I suppose one more episode from the life of Athena!

— That's right! In the centre of the west pediment was illustrated the dispute between Athena and Poseidon over the possession of the city. Next to the gods were depicted their gifts, the olive tree, that was possibly made of metal, and water flowing out of a rock at Poseidon's feet.

— Why did Athena offer the olive tree?

— This was a fabrication of the Athenians, because the olive tree was not only a characteristic plant of Attica, but also one of the most important trees in human history. So, by propagating that the goddess had offered them the olive tree, they claimed primacy in olive cultivation across the entire world, aiming to highlight the significance of Athens in culture.

Cephissus (?)   Erysichthon (?)   Cecrops-Pandrosos   Cecropids   Nike   Hermes   Chariot of Athena   Athen

— Why do the two gods draw back in surprise?

— Because high between them stroke the thunderbolt of Zeus, made of metal, that put an end to the quarrel. You can imagine how horrendous its sound must have been to frighten the two gods! Pheidias conceived this ingenious device to enliven the scene, capturing an impressive divine instant in an episode that sealed the fate of the city. To the left and right of the central composition, are shown the chariots of the two gods, whose horses also seem startled by the thunderclap.

— What about the rest of the figures? They don't seem too relevant to the main theme!

— It is true that the rest of the figures, men, women and children, are the families of the mythical heroes and ancient kings of the city, who acted as judges of the divine contest. Among them are portrayed the two divine messengers, Hermes and Iris, who carried to them information about the conflict. At the two ends we see two reclining male figures that symbolize the two rivers of Athens, Cephissus and Ilissos and probably the fountain Kallirrhoe.

Poseidon   Chariot of Poseidon   Iris   Amphitrite   Oreithyia with Kalais and Zetes   Ion (?)   Kreousa (?)   Praxithea (?)   Ilissos (?)   Kallirrhoe (?)

INTERPRETING THE PEDIMENTAL COMPOSITIONS

— Now, tell me, why did the Athenians choose these two subjects to decorate the Parthenon pediments?

— These two mythological episodes were selected by the temple's creators to convey specific messages: To begin with, what is emphasized is the presence and decisive role of Athena in the history of the city. From her birth on the east pediment, to her quarrel with Poseidon on the west, everything that happens between the gods is aimed at the glory of Athens.

Simultaneously, it is fascinating that in the Parthenon appear all gods, as they were on Mount Olympus, in the most resplendent depiction of the divine family in ancient art. The Athenians request the attention of all gods, because they feel they are at the centre of the world. They want to show that the gods are born, care for, participate in, and fight with each other for their beloved city.

— Wow!! Unbelievable! I never would have thought that Pheidias could succeed in uniting gods and men in such a manner!

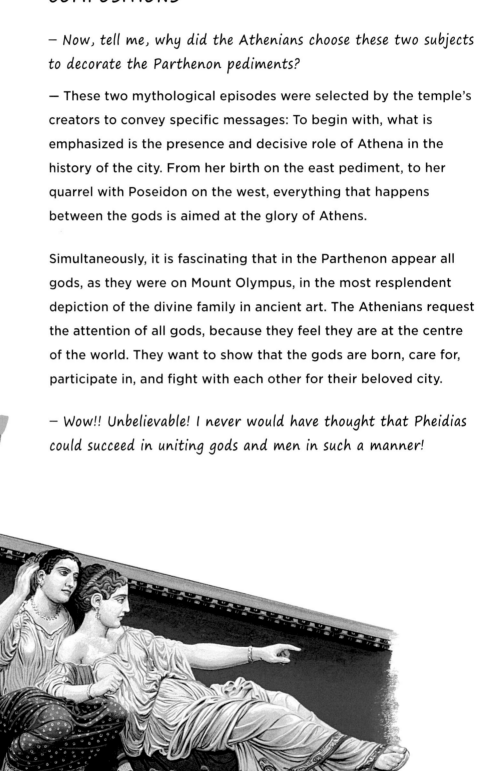

THE COLOURS OF THE MONUMENTS

— And this union became more vivid through the colours applied to the monuments.

— Indeed! In the reconstructions, we see that many parts of the temples as well as the sculptures were painted. Was it really like that?

— Yes, it was! The entire upper part of temples, above the epistyle, was polychrome. The triglyphs as well as the background of the pediments and the frieze were blue, while the background of the metopes was red. As for the figures, the flesh parts of men were painted light brown, whereas in female figures they were left white. In contrast, women's garments were marked by a variety of colours, thus turning the representations even more vibrant. This impressive image was further accentuated by individual elements, such as weapons, horse harnesses, female jewellery, symbols held by the gods, etc, which were made of gilt bronze.

CHRYSELEPHANTINE ATHENA

— I guess the chryselephantine statue of Athena Parthenos inside the temple was staggeringly colourful!

— I'm afraid it was not! It only featured ... two colours; white from the ivory and gold from the gold it was made of. However, it was enormous; it was 11.50 m tall, and its size and beauty inspired awe and wonder among the faithful. The work was created by Pheidias himself and, although he was assisted by a large team of sculptors and assistants, it took him several years to finish it.

— How do we know what it looked like? Has anything survived?

— No! We do know, however, what it looked like from detailed descriptions by ancient writers and also from around 200 later small copies and representations of it in every art form.

— How was the chryselephantine Athena made exactly?

— The statue consisted of a core made of wood and plaster onto which the goddess's face, arms and feet, made of ivory, were affixed. Her garments were made of gold plates, 1,150 kilos in weight, that, based on the construction technique, could be removed and reattached to their position.

— Is that so? Why did they do such thing? Did they take the gold off and hide it to protect it from theft?

— No, the Parthenon, like all temples, had heavy doors that locked and opened only a few days a year, during which people could enter the temple and pray before the goddess and concurrently admire the great work of art. The fact that the gold could be detached is known to us from an ancient account, according to which when a distrustful Athenian accused Pheidias of misappropriating part of the statue's gold, the sculptor removed it and weighed it in the presence of his accuser to prove that the allegation was groundless.

— I have heard that in front of the statue there was a basin filled with water. Is this true?

— Yes, it is. They believed that humidity was necessary for the good preservation state of the statue's ivory parts. However, the water may have also been employed to reflect light entering through the door, so as to improve the statue's illumination. I should remind you that the interior of temples was poorly lit, and this atmosphere would increase the sense of wonder felt by the worshippers before the goddess. In addition, the statue would be mirrored in the placid water creating impressive reflections!

A PARTHENON IN AMERICA

— In conclusion, please tell me: Did the Athenians actually accomplish their goal with all these monuments they built?

— Look! I believe that the vision of Pericles and his collaborators, as well as its implementation fulfilled their goal, which was to turn Athens into the leading city across the entire Greek world. The ancients themselves have admitted it. However, something more important occurred which they could not possibly imagine: These works transcended time and ages and became major landmarks in the history of civilization. That's something!

— It sure is!

— In fact, many of these monuments were copied in modern times, either in their entirety or as facades integrated into larger buildings. The most striking example is the full-scale replica of the Parthenon built of concrete in Nashville, Tennessee (USA). The monument was built between 1921 and 1931, while in 1990, an exact copy of the chryselephantine statue of Athena was installed in its interior, as we see on p. 75.

— Amazing!! I never would have thought that there would be a Parthenon standing on grass! But, why did the Acropolis turn into a symbol of Democracy?

— Because it was the work of all the Athenians! In contrast to works of other cultures, it was not intended to serve the glory of one ruler, nor its building was decided by himself to be obsequiously executed by his subjects. The work was the outcome of the common will and decision of all citizens, who consciously and actively participated in all stages of its implementation: From the voting process in the *Ekklesia tou Demou* (Assembly) for the acceptance of Pericles's programme, to the approval of its annual budget, as well as the monitoring of the work's progress from the first to the last day. Of course, a major democratic achievement is also the pride which they all felt for this glorious undertaking —pride that gave them self-confidence and faith in the power of their city.

SO OLD, YET SO MODERN

— Now that we are over, tell me in a few words, why, although all the things we discussed are so old, there is still a continuing interest in them today?

— Because the intellectual and material works produced by the people of this bygone era changed the course of history and remain alive to this day. A history that goes on uninterruptedly, enriched with the new and significant accomplishments of each epoch in all aspects of civilization which, not only facilitate people's lives, but offer them new possibilities to become better and to make their presence on earth meaningful.
Now that we are over ... can I ask you something?

— Sure!

— What do you think of our journey? Did you find it a bit ... tedious?

— It was fantastic ... !!!

THE ACROPOLIS HISTORY TIMELINE

3200 BC

The Acropolis and its surrounding area are settled.

13th CENTURY BC

The Cyclopean Mycenaean fortification and a palace are built.

8th CENTURY BC

Cult activity emerges and a small temple is erected.

448/7 BC

The Periclean building programme commences.

448/7–437 BC

The Parthenon is built.

437–431 BC

The Propylaea is constructed.

1687

The Parthenon is blown up by Morosini.

1801–1803

The monuments are looted by Lord Elgin.

1975

The last restoration programme is launched.

6th CENTURY BC

The first large temples are built of poros stone and statues are dedicated to the goddess.

508/7 BC

The Athenian Democracy is established.

480 BC

The Acropolis is destroyed by the Persians.

426–421 BC

The temple of Athena Nike is built.

421–413 and 409–406 BC

The Erechtheion is built.

4th CENTURY AD

The Parthenon metopes are destroyed.

2008

The Acropolis Museum is moved to its new building.

2009

The New Acropolis Museum is inaugurated.

BIBLIOGRAPHY

M. Korres, *From Pentelicon to the Parthenon* (1994)

P. Tournikiotis (ed.), *The Parthenon and its Impact in Modern Times* (1994)

I. Trianti, *Acropolis Museum* (1998)

K. Hatziaslani, *Parthenon Promenades* (2000)

B. Holzmann, *L'Acropole d'Athènes. Monuments, cultes, et histoire du sanctuaire d'Athena Polias* (2003)

J. Hurwit, *The Acropolis in the Age of Pericles* (2004)

P. Valavanis, *Games and Sanctuaries in Ancient Greece. Olympia, Pythia, Isthmia, Nemea, Panathenaia* (2004), 281–333

J. Neils (ed.), *The Parthenon from Antiquity to the Present* (2005)

F. Mallouchou, The vicissitudes of the Athenian Acropolis in the 19th century, from castle to monument, in P. Valavanis (ed.), *Great Moments in Greek Archaeology* (2007) 36–57

Chr. Vlassopoulou, *The Athenian Acropolis, The Monuments and the Museum* (2007)

M. Korres et alii, *Dialogues on the Acropolis. Scholars and Experts talk on the History, Restoration and the Acropolis Museum* (2010)

D. Pandermalis, St. Eleftheratou, Chr. Vlassopoulou, *Acropolis Museum. Guide* (2014)

P. Valavanis, *The Acropolis through its Museum* (2014)

P. Valavanis, The Acropolis, in J. Neils, D. Rogers (eds), *The Cambridge Companion to Ancient Athens* (2021) 63–85

LIST OF FIGURES

CREATIVE DIRECTOR: MOSES KAPON
ARTISTIC DESIGNER: RACHEL MISDRAHI-KAPON
EDITING BY: DIMITRIOS DOUMAS
DTP: ELENI VALMA, MINA MANTA, EVGENIA STASSINAKI
PROCESSING OF ILLUSTRATIONS: MICHALIS TZANNETAKIS
BINDING: J. MANTIS & SONS L.P.